Children's Favorite
Bible Stories

TIME® LIFE BOOKS

Time-Life Books, Alexandria, Virginia

CONTENTS

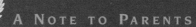

A NOTE TO PARENTS

Nature offers ideal opportunities to share God with children, and this story can be a good starting point. After reading it, you might sit under the stars and talk about how God created the stars and the moon. Listen to bird calls and begin to recognize each one. Give thanks that God made the world in colors, not black and white.

Since young children think concretely, they often ask us why they can't see God. You might ask a child how we know when the wind blows. We don't see the wind, but we hear it, feel its coolness, and see what it does. In the same way, we don't see God, but we feel God is near us and hear and see what God has made.

Scripture sources: **Genesis 1:1-27**

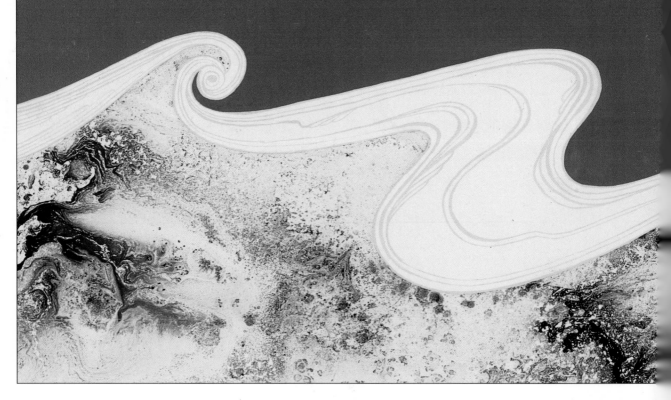

IN THE BEGINNING

Retold by Mary Quattlebaum

Illustrated by Bryn Barnard

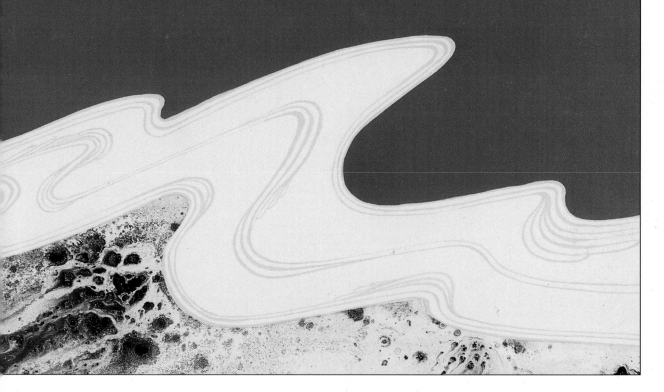

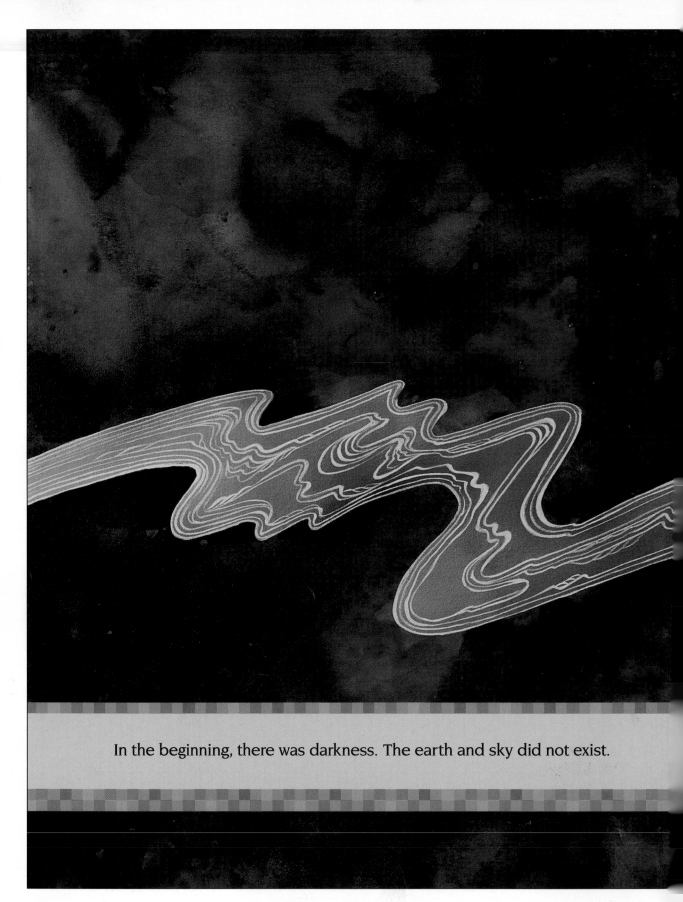

In the beginning, there was darkness. The earth and sky did not exist.

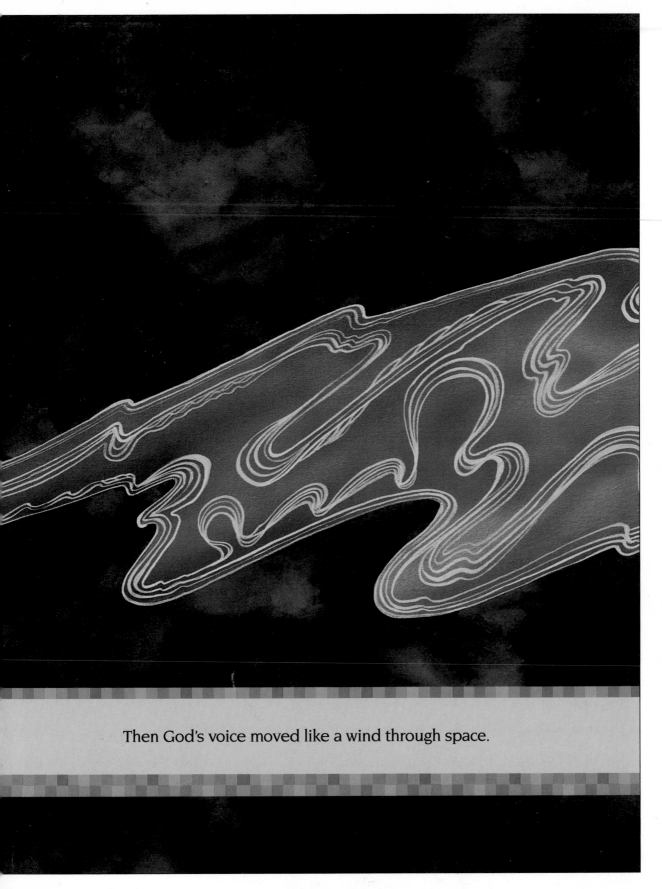

Then God's voice moved like a wind through space.

God said, "Let there be light," and the first light shone.

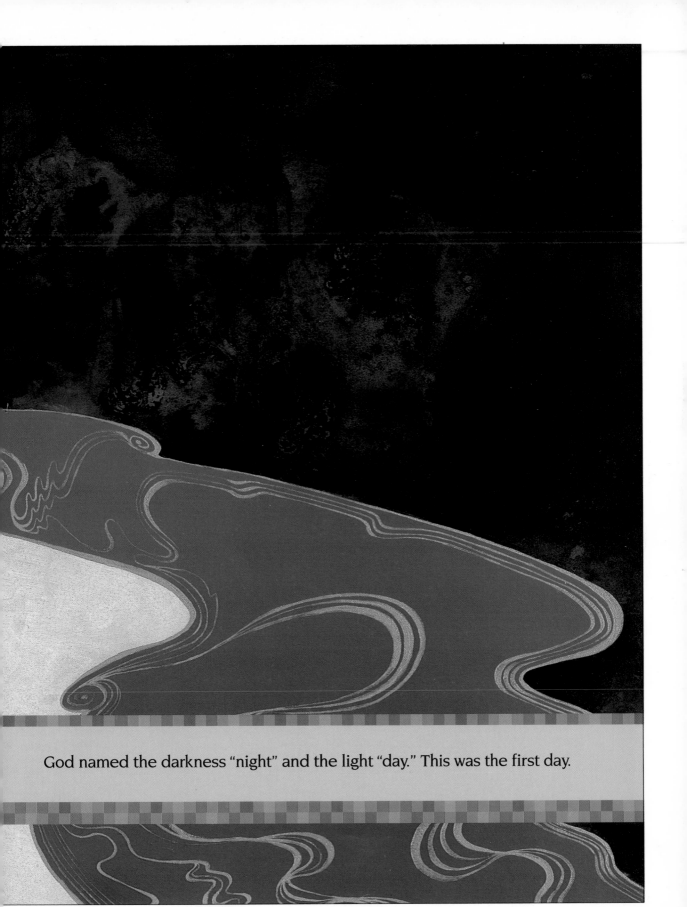

God named the darkness "night" and the light "day." This was the first day.

Then God created the sky.

The blue sky glowed above the dark waters. This was the second day.

From the waters, God created dry land.

God called the land "earth" and the water "seas."

"Let there be plants and trees," God said next.
Grass and flowering trees sprang into being.

Seeds sent out roots and grew. The earth filled with new green leaves and the sea with waving weeds. This was the third day.

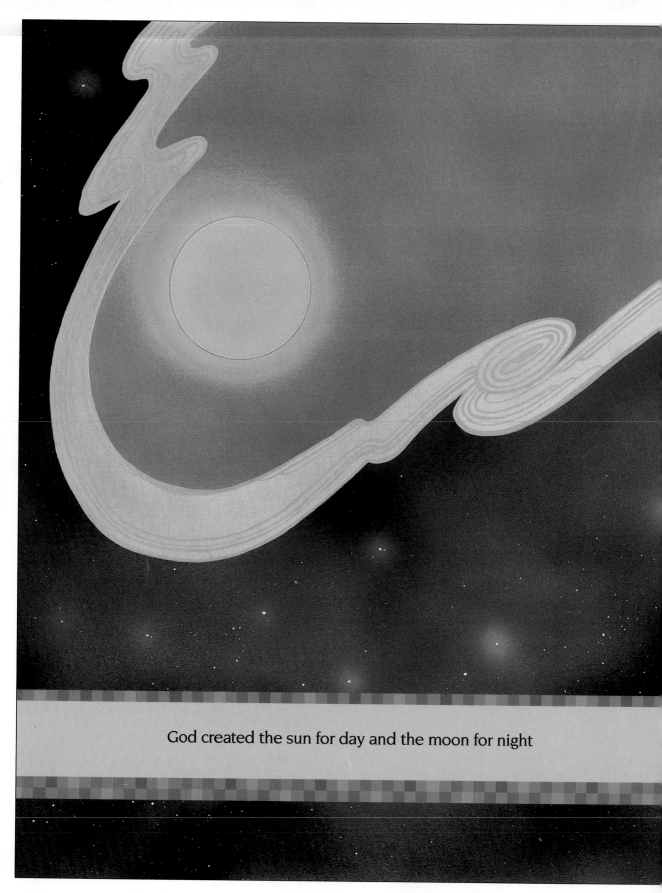

God created the sun for day and the moon for night

and set each star in the sky.

"These great lights will mark the seasons," God said.

This was the fourth day.

Next God created big fish and small fish and every kind of bird. The seas

filled with silvery life and the sky with singing birds. This was the fifth day.

"Let there be living creatures on the earth," God called. And animals raced through the grass and climbed the new trees.

Gazelles sprang into the air. Lizards napped on sun-warmed stones.
Frogs hopped in moonlit mud.

Then God created one man and one woman.
Sitting up, they smiled at the busy world.
　"Watch over the fish and birds," God told them.

"Take care of the sun and moon, the land and sea and sky.
You may use these things, but you must also protect them."
God blessed the man and woman. This was the sixth day.

On the seventh day, God rested. God looked at the man and woman, the bears and butterflies, the minnows, the whales, the plants.

One by one, God counted the stars.

The world stretched out, a beautiful place.

And God saw that it was good.

A Note to Parents

We often consider humankind's sinfulness to be the main theme of this story because Adam and Eve disobeyed God's command. However, woven into the story is a bright thread of God's loving care for us, even when we disobey. We have made sure that this telling of the story focuses on God's caring acts, such as providing the garden and giving Adam and Eve clothing when they must leave the garden. We do not want to burden children at such a young age with the "sinfulness of all humankind."

You might point out that Adam and Eve had a choice of whether or not to eat the fruit, and that God loved them even though they made the wrong choice. The Bible does not specify exactly what the fruit looked like, therefore we have chosen to make it unlike any fruits that children will know.

Help your child imagine how lovely the garden might have been. You can then discuss how caring for the environment helps God make our world a lovelier place. You might also talk about how the earth produces better food and plant life when we take care of it.

Scripture sources: **Genesis 2 and 3**

ADAM AND EVE

Retold by Mary Martin

Illustrated by Bryn Barnard

God created heaven and earth
and all the animals. Then God
created a man and named the
man Adam. God put Adam in a
beautiful garden in a place
called Eden. All different kinds
of trees and flowers grew there.
A sparkling river ran through
the garden, bringing water to all
the living things.

God said to Adam, "This is your home. It is sunny and warm. Its trees are filled with food. You can eat fruit from any tree, but do not eat the fruit from the tree that grows in the middle of the garden. For this is the tree of knowledge of good and evil."

Then God brought all the animals to Adam. God said,
"Give each animal a name."

Adam looked carefully at each one and then he named it.

God did not want Adam to be alone, so God created a woman. She would be a companion for Adam and live

with him in the garden of Eden. Adam named her Eve.

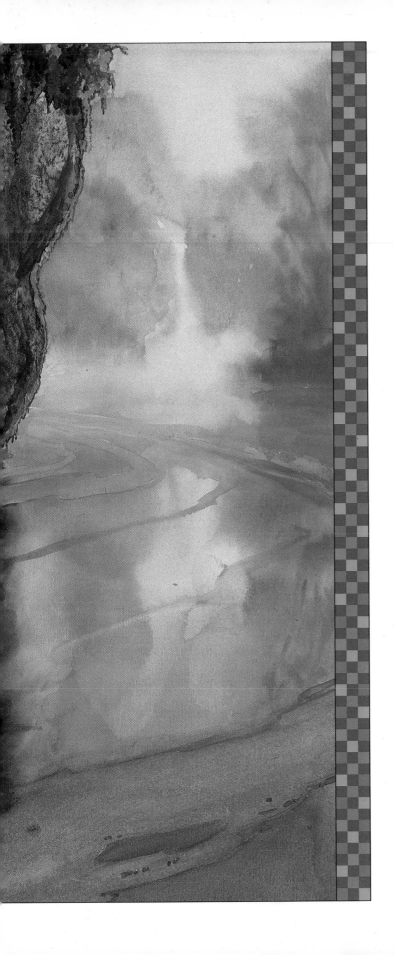

Adam and Eve lived happily
in the garden. They swam in
the river and played with the
animals. They cared for the
trees and flowers that grew
there. They always had
enough to eat. They ate fruits
from all the different trees in
the garden. But they did not
eat fruit from the tree of
knowledge.

Then one day, Eve saw a
serpent in the tree of
knowledge.

"Eat the fruit of this tree,"
the serpent said.

"But God told us not to," Eve
said. "Surely, God knows what
is best."

"Nothing will happen to you.
The fruit of this tree will make
you as wise as God," said the
serpent. "You will know
everything."

Eve listened to the words of the serpent. As she looked at
the delicious fruit, she forgot the words of God.

She picked a fruit and ate it. Then she gave some to Adam.
He ate it, too.

Immediately, they felt very sorry. What would God say?

They hid behind a tree, but God saw them and asked, "Why do you hide? Did you eat the fruit from the tree of knowledge?"

"Yes," whispered Adam and Eve.

"You disobeyed me," God said. God was sad.

Because Adam and Eve had eaten the fruit, they now knew the difference between good and evil. They knew the difference between right and wrong. They knew they had done wrong when they disobeyed God.

Then God said to Adam and Eve, "Because you disobeyed me, you must leave this beautiful garden."

Adam and Eve were very sorry and they cried as they left.

The world outside the garden of Eden was very different. It was
not always sunny and warm. Because God loved them, God

wanted to protect Adam and Eve even though they had
disobeyed. So God gave them clothes to keep them warm.

Adam and Eve made a new home in the land
beyond the garden. They grew their own food.
They worked hard and felt hunger and pain. But
they felt joy, too.

They thanked God for all the good things in the
world. They asked God for protection. And God
continued to watch over Adam and Eve.

A Note to Parents

This story has long been a favorite with children, primarily because they enjoy reading about animals. This version emphasizes the care and love that Noah and his family gave to animals, and tells how Noah followed God's instruction to build a large boat and help his family and the animals ride out the storm. Because young children have a limited ability to think abstractly, the story does not dwell on abstract concepts of wickedness or judgement.

As you read this story, you might remind your children of times that you care for animals too. Use the story again and again as you enjoy animals, as you watch the rain on the windowpane, and as you experience a rainbow.

Scripture sources: **Genesis 6:9 through 9:17**

Noah's Ark

Retold by Patricia Daniels

Illustrated by Kathy Rusynyk

Many years ago, in a faraway land, there lived a wise old farmer named Noah. Noah was a good man, and he and his family lived a peaceful life. They grew grapes and figs in the warmth of the sun and took care of their animals with gentle hands.

One day, when Noah was tending his trees, he heard the voice of God.

"Noah," said God, "a great flood is coming. I want you to build a huge boat, an ark. Then bring onto the ark two of every kind of animal in the world. Your family and these creatures will be safe from the flood."

Noah did what God asked. From all around the land he
brought in stacks of sweet-smelling cypress wood.

Day after day, he and his sons, Shem, Ham, and Japheth,

hammered and nailed the planks of the ark.

Finally the enormous boat was finished. A wooden ramp led up to the open doors. As Noah put away his tools, his son Shem called to him.

"Father," he cried, "look out there!"

Noah turned around. Down every road, over every hill, animals big and small appeared. Birds filled the air. Ants and ladybugs and spiders scurried along the ground.

With a rumble of footsteps and a rush of wings the animals entered the ark. Elephants stomped up the steep ramp. Jack rabbits leaped. Swallows swooped overhead. Noah's family watched while a male and female of every animal on earth found a place aboard the ark.

The inside of the ark was busy as animals settled in on beds of straw.

Noah felt a light touch on his shoulder. It was a shy white dove, leaning close to him. "Don't worry, little one," he said, stroking its neck. Then he raised his head to listen. The first drops of rain were rattling against the side of the ark.

It rained and rained and rained. Water lifted the ark from
the ground. Floating on the flood, the ark rose above

the trees. Then it rose above the highest

mountains. The rain fell for 40 days and 40 nights.

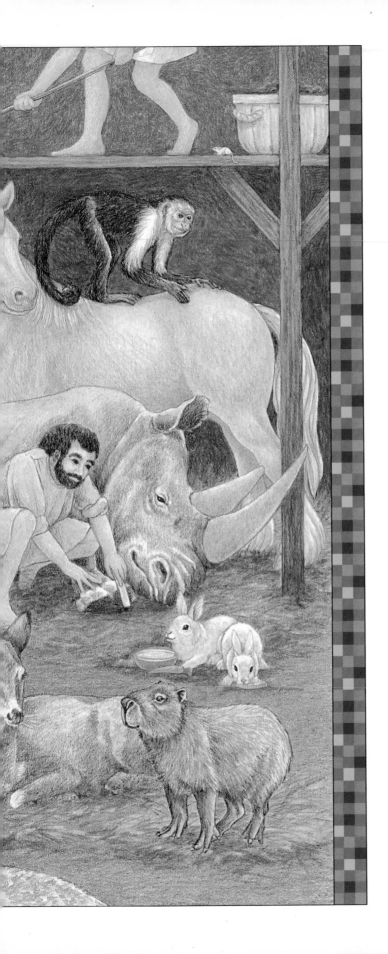

The animals felt safe inside the ark as it rode the waters. Noah's family fed and bathed them. Shem scratched the pigs' backs when they were itchy. Japheth filed the rhinos' toenails when they got too long. The little dove went everywhere on Noah's shoulder.

Finally, the rain stopped. The water grew calm. Sunlight shone on the wet deck of the ark.

Noah opened a window. "Go, little friend," he said to the dove. "Fly away and look for land."

The dove returned hours later, tired and sad. Noah let it rest for a week. Then he sent it out again. This time the dove came back joyfully, with an olive leaf in its beak.

"Land!" cried Noah. "Bless you, small one!"

As the water began to drain away, Noah saw that the
ark was resting on the side of a mountain. Trees and fields
appeared below them. When the land was dry, Noah

opened the ark's wide doors. In pairs and in families,
the animals left the boat. They ran and flew and slithered
into the sunny valley below.

A glorious rainbow swept
across the sky above the ark.
God spoke again to Noah.

"This rainbow is a sign,"
God said. "I promise that a
flood will never again cover
the whole earth."

And Noah and his family
and two free-flying doves
settled down in the valley.
They lived happily afterward
through rain and shine.

A Note to Parents

The description of Joseph's coat varies depending on which translation of the biblical text is used. Early English translations called it a "coat of many colors," which is the version we've chosen to follow. However, more modern translations suggest it might have been a long coat with long or big sleeves. In either case, the description indicates the coat was luxurious for that time.

To make this story appropriate for young children, the more complex parts of the biblical text have been left out. For example, we do not describe the various dreams Joseph interpreted. Nor do we point out that Joseph and Benjamin were half brothers to Jacob's other sons. Such details can be added as your child grows older and is able to understand them.

This retelling focuses on the lesson of forgiveness and shows how God can make something good come out of a bad situation. You might point out to your child how wrong Joseph's brothers were to treat him so harshly, but how good Joseph was to forgive them.

Scripture sources: **Genesis 37–50**

Joseph and the Coat of Many Colors

Retold by Andrew Gutelle

Illustrated by Bill Farnsworth

A very long time ago, in a land called Canaan, there lived a man named Jacob. He had twelve sons. Although he loved them all, his son Joseph was very special to him. Jacob gave Joseph a gift. It was a brightly-colored coat made from the finest wool.

Joseph's older brothers took care of their father's sheep. Their clothes were rough and dull. The sight of Joseph in his soft, rainbow-colored coat made them very angry.

One day, the older brothers were tending sheep far away from home. Jacob sent Joseph to find them and make sure they were safe and well.

The brothers saw Joseph walking toward them in his coat of many colors. They noticed how the sunlight made his beautiful coat sparkle. With every step Joseph took, his brothers became more and more angry.

Some of Joseph's brothers even wanted to kill him. But Reuben, the oldest brother, said, "We cannot kill him. Why not put him into this deep pit and leave him there?" Reuben secretly planned to come back later and rescue Joseph from the pit.

The brothers agreed. They grabbed Joseph, tore off his coat, and then threw him into the pit. Joseph cried out to his brothers for help, but they would not listen.

85

Later that day, when Reuben was away, the brothers saw some traders traveling by. The brothers took Joseph from the pit and sold him to the

traders who were on their way to the land of Egypt. When Reuben
returned and found his brother was gone, he was very sad.

"Our father must never know what we have done," said one of the brothers.

So they took Joseph's beautiful coat and smeared it with blood from a goat. Then they took it home to their father.

"Oh, no!" cried Jacob when he saw Joseph's coat. "A wild animal has attacked and killed Joseph." Jacob cried and his sons said nothing.

But Joseph was not dead. He was living in Egypt. The traders had sold Joseph to a rich man to be his slave. Joseph worked very hard and had faith that God was taking care of him and someday things would change.

At last that day came. Pharaoh, the king of Egypt, sent for Joseph. "You are only a slave," said Pharaoh, "but people say you are wise. I am troubled by my dreams. You must help me understand them."

Joseph listened, knowing that God would help him to understand. Pharaoh told him one dream and then another.

"A terrible time is coming," Joseph said when Pharaoh finished. "A time when no food will grow. You must prepare so your people will not starve."

Pharaoh was pleased. "You are no longer a slave, Joseph," he said.
"You shall work with me to prepare for the hard times ahead. Begin
collecting the food at once!"

For seven years, Joseph gathered food. When the hard times
came, Egypt was ready. The people did not go
hungry and Joseph became rich and powerful.

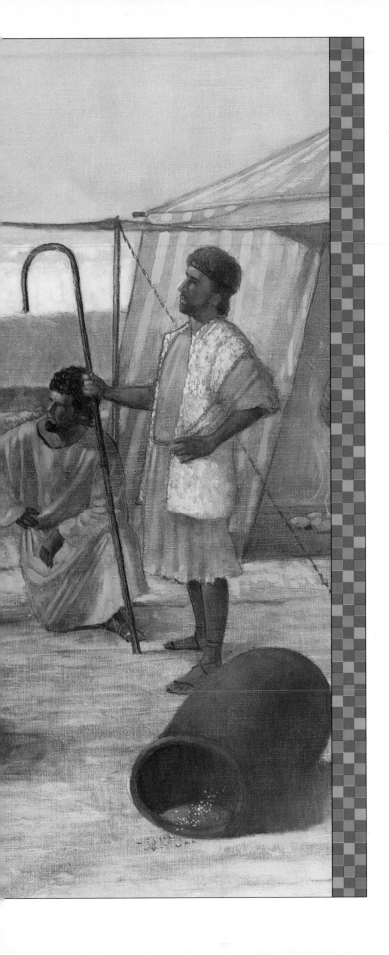

But when hard times came to Joseph's father and brothers, they did not have enough food. They heard there was plenty of food in Egypt, so Jacob told his sons to go there and buy some food to bring back to their families. Only Benjamin, the youngest, stayed at home.

When the brothers reached Egypt, they went to
see the man in charge of selling food. They did not
know this man was their brother Joseph. They did
not recognize him because now he was older and
wearing fine clothes. Joseph welcomed his brothers
into his house and sold them the food they
needed. But he did not tell them who he was.

The brothers went home, but soon they needed more food. When they returned to Joseph, they brought their youngest brother, Benjamin, who was Joseph's favorite. Joseph was so happy to see all his brothers again that he couldn't keep his secret any longer. He told them who he was.

His brothers were very sorry for what they had done to him. They were also afraid that Joseph would punish them.

"Now do not get upset or blame yourselves because you sold me to the traders," Joseph said. "It was really God who sent me here to make sure the people of Egypt would have food to eat."

Joseph asked his brothers to come live with him in Egypt. He told them to bring their families and their father, Jacob.

When Jacob got to Egypt, he saw his long lost son.

Joyfully, he said, "This is a day I dreamed of."

From that day on, Joseph and all his family lived in peace and happiness.

A NOTE TO PARENTS

David and Goliath is probably a story from your own childhood; perhaps the courage of David attracted you to the tale. Today's children see violence at every turn of the television knob. Rather than dwelling on the violence in this story, focus on the person of David.

In all likelihood, David was a teenager responsible for taking care of sheep alone after his bar mitzvah at age thirteen. Young children enjoy looking up to youths as role models. Talk about the earlier part of David's life. Point out how David helped his father and played music that made King Saul feel better. Encourage your child to think of ways that he or she can be helpful, like David.

You might also talk about how David must have practiced using his sling so that he could protect the sheep. David knew that God would help him since he had practiced. Talk about special things that your child has learned to do, and thank God for those things.

Scripture sources: **1 Samuel 16:14-17:49**

DAVID AND GOLIATH

Retold by Andrew Gutelle

Illustrated by Bill Farnsworth

David was a boy who lived a long, long time ago in the city of Bethlehem.

He was the youngest--and smallest--of eight brothers. It was David who

looked after his father's sheep. When he was not working, he played music

on his lyre. The people of Bethlehem said it was beautiful music.

One morning, as his sheep searched for sweet bits of grass, David saw a man coming up the road. What could this stranger want?

"I bring greetings from King Saul of Israel," said the man. "Our king's heart is filled with sadness. He asks you to come and play music to cheer him."

That day David set out on his father's donkey. He rode to the home of the king.

King Saul watched as he strummed the strings of his lyre. He listened as the boy sang. Then, finally, the king smiled.

"Your music brightens my home," said the king happily. He asked David to stay with him. The boy lived with King Saul for many months, soothing him with music.

Then, one day, a messenger came. An army of
Philistines was marching toward the land of Israel.
King Saul left to lead his soldiers into battle. He
sent young David home to his father.

When David arrived, he saw the two armies facing each other across a
wide valley. In the middle of the valley stood David's brothers with some
other soldiers. They were looking at a giant man in glittering armor.

When David arrived, he saw the two armies facing each other across a
wide valley. In the middle of the valley stood David's brothers with some
other soldiers. They were looking at a giant man in glittering armor.

Then, one day, a messenger came. An army of
Philistines was marching toward the land of Israel.
King Saul left to lead his soldiers into battle. He
sent young David home to his father.

Three of David's brothers had joined Saul's army. David's father worried about them. One morning, he called his youngest son.

"David, take this bread and cheese to your brothers," said his father. "See that they are well."

He was the biggest person anyone had ever seen.

"The armies do not need to fight," roared the giant. "Two people can settle this. Send out your best warrior, and I, Goliath, will defeat him!"

King Saul could not argue with the boy's faith. He gave David the king's own suit of armor. It was so heavy the boy could barely stand up. Saul's long sword dragged against the ground.

"I cannot walk with these," said David to King Saul. He took off the armor and put on his own simple clothes.

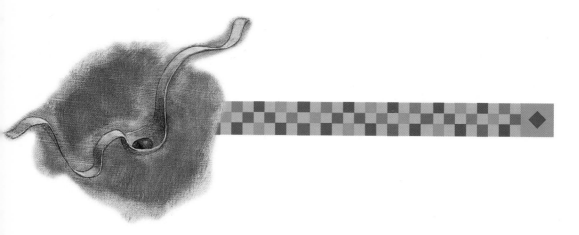

Nobody dared to fight Goliath—nobody except David. He hurried to see the king.

"You are just a boy. You have no chance against that monster of a man," said King Saul. "How can you possibly defeat him?"

"When a lion or bear used to come after my sheep," replied David, "I would strike it down with a stone from my sling. God, who protected me from the paw of the lion and the bear, will save me from the hand of Goliath."

King Saul could not argue with the boy's faith. He gave David the king's own suit of armor. It was so heavy the boy could barely stand up. Saul's long sword dragged against the ground.

"I cannot walk with these," said David to King Saul. He took off the armor and put on his own simple clothes.

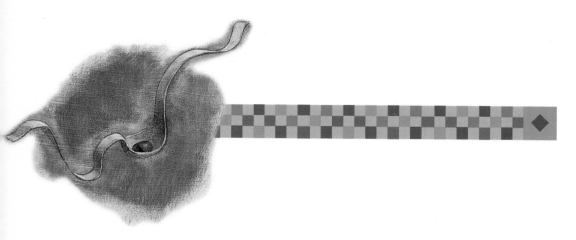

He was the biggest person anyone had ever seen.

"The armies do not need to fight," roared the giant. "Two people can settle this. Send out your best warrior, and I, Goliath, will defeat him!"

David took his sling and went
to meet Goliath. Along the way
he stopped by a stream.
Reaching into the cool water, he
picked up five smooth stones.
He dried each one and put
them all in his leather pouch.

In the valley, Goliath was waiting. The armies stood watching. Slowly,

David stepped forward from the soldiers. He was holding his sling.

When Goliath saw him, he laughed so hard that his armor rattled. "Am I a dog," he shouted to David, "that you come to me with sticks?"

David reached into his pouch and took out one stone. He placed it in his sling and spun it round and round.

With all his might, David let go and sent the stone whistling through the air. It struck Goliath in the forehead. For an instant, the giant stood silently. Then he came crashing to the ground.

David ran forward. He picked up Goliath's sword and held it high above his head. The soldiers in Goliath's army turned and ran away, chased by the soldiers of Israel.

And David? He smiled. He knew that God did not care who was big, or who had the most armor. God was with him because he had trusted God.

A NOTE TO PARENTS

This story is about a man's attempt to run away from the responsibilities given to him by God. The story teaches us that God accepts and forgives us even when we behave badly if we are truly sorry for what we have done.

In telling this story for young children, we have purposely avoided some concepts we feel are too mature for them to grasp, such as the sinfulness of the people of Nineveh and Jonah's anger with God for not destroying the city.

The biblical account simply says that Jonah was swallowed by a big fish. We have chosen to follow the traditional representation of the creature as a whale.

Scripture source: **Jonah**

JONAH AND THE WHALE

Retold *by* Melissa Nichols

Illustrated by Christa Kieffer

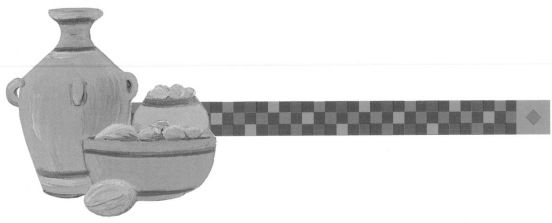

Once, long ago, there was a big city named
Nineveh. God watched over the people who
lived there. But God was not happy with
them for often the people did things that
did not please God.

But Jonah disobeyed God and did not take the message to Nineveh. Instead he ran away and tried to hide from God. He traveled to a harbor where he found a ship that was sailing to a place far away. Jonah got on the ship and sailed off.

God asked a man named Jonah to take a message to the people of Nineveh.

Jonah heard the voice of God say, "Go to Nineveh, that great city, and tell everyone that I am not pleased with the things they are doing."

But Jonah disobeyed God and did not take the message to Nineveh. Instead he ran away and tried to hide from God. He traveled to a harbor where he found a ship that was sailing to a place far away. Jonah got on the ship and sailed off.

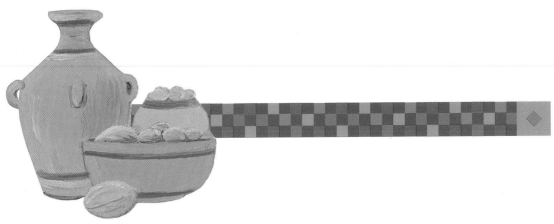

Once, long ago, there was a big city named
Nineveh. God watched over the people who
lived there. But God was not happy with
them for often the people did things that
did not please God.

Once at sea, a mighty storm began. Rain poured from the sky.
Great waves shook the ship.

Powerful winds beat against its sails with such force that the
ship was in danger of being torn apart.

Each of the sailors prayed that the ship would make it safely through the storm. They threw things overboard to make the ship lighter so that it might float more easily. But nothing helped.

Jonah was sound asleep below the deck and didn't know the ship was in danger. The captain of the ship was surprised when he found Jonah sleeping.

He awakened him and said, "How can you sleep at a time like this? Get up and pray! Perhaps God will be kind to us and we will not die at sea."

Jonah followed the captain's orders and then hurried up to the deck to help the sailors.

"Why are we having this terrible storm?" the sailors wanted to know.

Jonah was sure the storm was God's way of making him go to Nineveh. "This storm is because of me," he said. "God asked me to do something, but instead I ran away."

The men were very frightened by his words and by the storm that was growing wilder and wilder.

"What can we do to make the storm end?" the sailors asked.

Jonah told the men that the only thing to do was to toss him into the sea. They didn't want to throw Jonah overboard, but soon the sea became even more stormy. Finally, the sailors decided they had no choice and threw Jonah into the sea.

Once Jonah was in the water, the sea became calm. Jonah could see the ship sailing off in the distance.

To save Jonah from drowning, God sent a huge fish

148

to swallow him. Jonah stayed in the belly of that fish for three days and three nights. There he prayed to God for forgiveness and asked God to help him.

Hearing Jonah's prayers, God spoke to the huge
fish and soon the fish tossed Jonah out onto the
shore. There he heard the voice of God again
tell him to go to Nineveh. This time Jonah was
ready to do what God asked.

151

Jonah traveled to Nineveh. For three days he walked through the
great city. To everyone he saw he shouted God's warning, "In forty
days, Nineveh shall be destroyed if you do not change."

The people listened to Jonah. They understood his message. They knew that God was not pleased with the things they had done.

The people were sorry and quickly changed their ways. God was pleased. God forgave them and did not destroy the beautiful city of Ninevah.

A NOTE TO PARENTS

Feel free to share *The Story of Baby Jesus* with children not only during the Christmas season, but also throughout the year; this story can be a special story at any time. As you prepare to give gifts, remember that the wise men brought gifts for Jesus. Instead of concentrating on what gifts children will receive, ask them what they plan to give to others and help them anticipate how happy the gift will make the other person. And if you have the opportunity, arrange to visit a small baby. Read stories about Jesus as a man and talk about how he was the baby that we remember at Christmas.

Scripture sources: **Luke 1: 26-34 2:1-20 Matthew 2:1-12**

THE STORY OF BABY JESUS

Retold by Patricia Daniels

Illustrated by Sue Ellen Brown

Long, long ago, there was a little town called Nazareth. Nazareth lay in low, rolling hills a day's journey from the sea. In this quiet town lived a quiet young woman named Mary and a man named Joseph.

One day, as Mary sat sewing, the room filled with a clear, yet colorful light, like the inside of a diamond. In this light stood the angel Gabriel.

Mary was frightened, but Gabriel smiled kindly.

"Don't be afraid, Mary," he said. "God has chosen you to have a special child. You will name him Jesus, and he will be called the son of God."

"I will do as God says," said Mary.

And with a whoosh! of his great wings the angel disappeared.

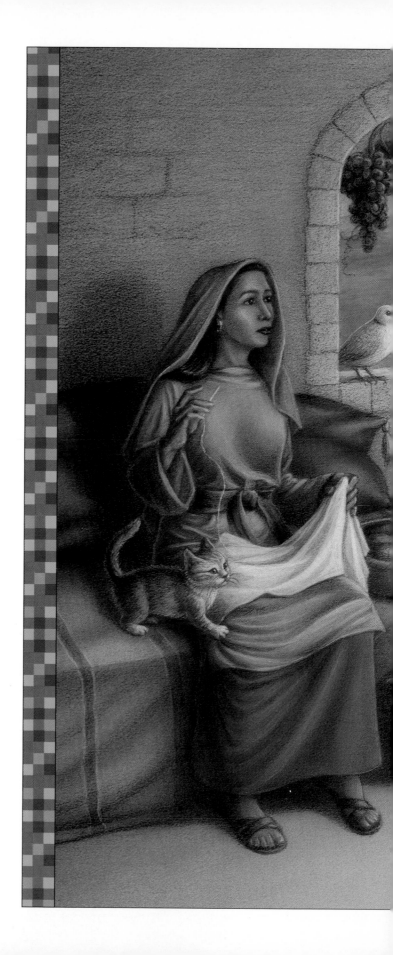

Months passed as Mary waited for her special baby
to be born. One day, Mary and Joseph had to go to
the town of Bethlehem, many miles away. Together
they packed clothes and food onto the back of
Joseph's donkey, Susannah. On a windy morning
they set out.

The journey took three long,
dusty days. Mary rode on the
donkey's back. Joseph walked
beside them. Susannah kept
her head down and thought
about a warm stable at the end
of the journey. As the third day
darkened into night, they saw
the lights of Bethlehem ahead.

"Joseph," said Mary,
"I think the baby's coming."

Joseph could see that many people were visiting Bethlehem. He went to the first inn that he saw.

"Innkeeper," he said to the man who opened the door, "please find us a room for the night. We are tired and expecting a baby."

But the innkeeper just shook his head. "There is no room at this inn," he said. "Nor at any other inn in Bethlehem."

The innkeeper was right. Joseph and Mary went
from inn to inn, but there was no room for them.
Then Susannah snorted and nudged Joseph with
her nose. The donkey led them to a stable
at the edge of town.

The stable door was open. The cows and sheep
inside looked at them with friendly brown eyes.
Joseph helped Mary lie down on a bed of straw.

Outside, in the grassy hills around Bethlehem, shepherds huddled in their coats and watched their sheep.

Suddenly, an angel appeared in the sky. Light shone on the surprised faces of the shepherds.

"I bring you good news!" said the angel in a singing voice. "Today the promised child has been born. You will find him lying in a manger, wrapped in bands of cloth."

And the angel was joined in the starry sky by other glorious angels singing praises to God.

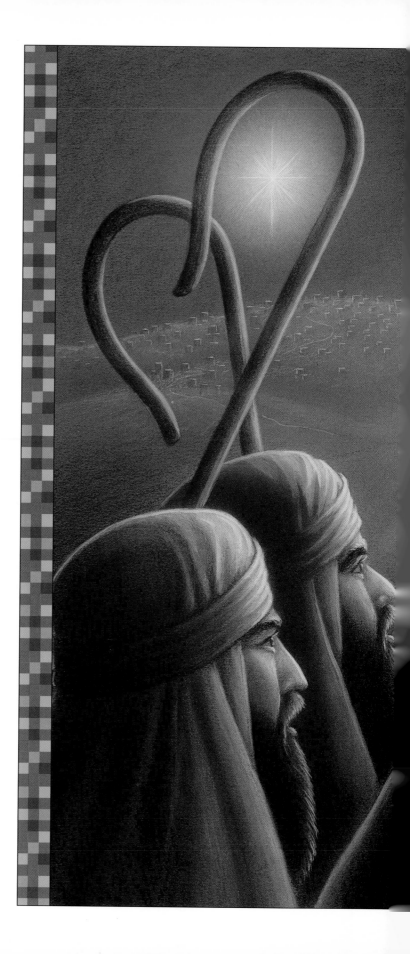

The innkeeper was right. Joseph and Mary went
from inn to inn, but there was no room for them.
Then Susannah snorted and nudged Joseph with
her nose. The donkey led them to a stable
at the edge of town.

The stable door was open. The cows and sheep
inside looked at them with friendly brown eyes.
Joseph helped Mary lie down on a bed of straw.

And it was there in a stable, on a starry night, that Mary gave birth
to a beautiful boy. She and Joseph loved him.

They wrapped the baby in bands of cloth so he would feel warm
and safe. Then they laid him in the animals' manger to sleep.

Outside, in the grassy hills around Bethlehem, shepherds huddled in their coats and watched their sheep.

Suddenly, an angel appeared in the sky. Light shone on the surprised faces of the shepherds.

"I bring you good news!" said the angel in a singing voice. "Today the promised child has been born. You will find him lying in a manger, wrapped in bands of cloth."

And the angel was joined in the starry sky by other glorious angels singing praises to God.

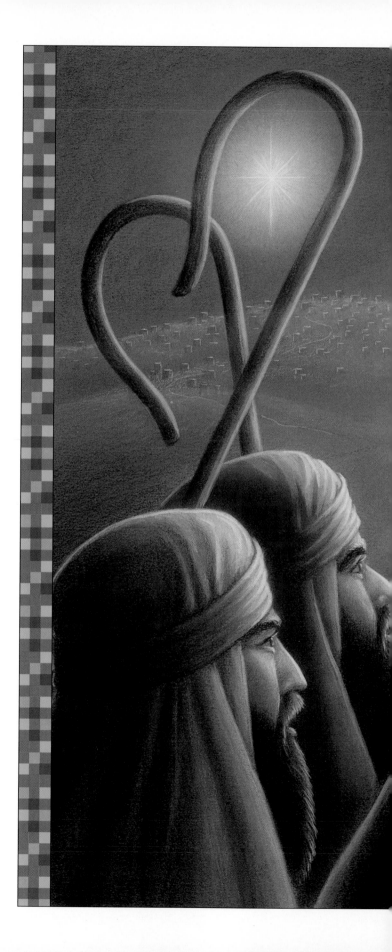

When the angels had gone, the shepherds hurried down from the hills to the tiny stable. There they saw the child resting in the straw.

"Father!" said the first shepherd boy. "The baby smiled at me!" The boy smiled back, his heart filled with happiness. Then he took his father's hand and left to spread the joyful news through the town.

As the days passed, people in Bethlehem and beyond
began to hear about the holy child. Mary, Joseph, and the baby
moved into a small house and received many visitors.

One night they had the most amazing guests of all: three
wise men on camelback, bringing presents of gold and perfumes
for the growing child.

"How did you find us?" Mary asked the wise men.

"We were told to follow the great star," they answered, pointing to the sky.

Mary and Joseph looked up. It was true—a splendid star lit up the sky above their house.

"What is the baby's name?" the wise men asked.

"Jesus," said Mary and Joseph proudly.

Jesus Christ grew up to be a great teacher who would tell people about faith and love. To this day, 2,000 years later, people around the world celebrate his birthday on Christmas.

A NOTE TO PARENTS

Although this parable is commonly known as "The Prodigal Son," the moral of the story is really about the love and forgiveness of the father, not the waywardness of the son. In biblical times, if a son denounced his heritage, as the young son does in this story, the father would consider him dead and never have contact with him again. Jesus challenges that social norm by having the father eagerly await the son's return, ready to forgive, behavior which most people of that time would have thought disgraceful.

Help your child understand that like a parent, God loves the child even when the child has done wrong. This type of love is sometimes called "grace." As you correct children's wrongdoings, let them know that even though you do not like their actions, you still love them. In this way you are modeling after the loving grace of God.

Scripture sources: **Luke 15:11-32**

THE PRODIGAL SON

Retold by David Michaels

Illustrated by Steve Cieslawski

Jesus once told a story about a man who lived on a beautiful farm with his two sons. The father loved both boys very much. He promised his sons that everything he owned was theirs to share.

The younger son was not happy on the farm. He dreamed of an exciting life far away. One day, he went to his father and said, "You once told me that half of everything you have is mine. I want my half now so I can leave home and have fun."

The father was very sad. He didn't want his son to
leave. But, knowing that he could not make him stay,
the father agreed to give the younger son his share

of the money. And soon after, the son packed up all
his things and left home. He went to a country far away.

At first the son was very happy. He had fun every day. He thought he was rich, so he was not careful with his money and spent it in foolish ways. He made lots of new friends and bought them fancy meals and other expensive things.

Before long, the son found that all his money was gone. He had spent it all. He looked to his new friends for help. Since he had no more money, they would not help him.

Then a famine spread through the country. Food was hard to find and soon the son had nothing to eat. Poor and hungry, the boy thought to himself, "I must find a job."

So off he went in search of work.

189

The only job the son could find was feeding pigs for a farmer. As he gave the pigs their food, he wished he had something to eat, too. But no one gave him any food.

"If only I were home," he wished as he remembered all the good things there. "Everyone eats well. Even the servants have plenty to eat."

He missed his father and brother very much. But he was afraid to go home. What if his father didn't love him anymore?

Finally he decided, "I will return home and tell my father that I know I was wrong and I'm very sorry. If he'll forgive me, maybe he will at least let me be a servant in his house."

To show that he forgave his son, the father called his servants and said, "Quickly, bring out a robe—the best one—and put it on him. Put a ring on his finger and sandals on his feet."

Then the father ordered that a great feast be prepared to celebrate his younger son's return.

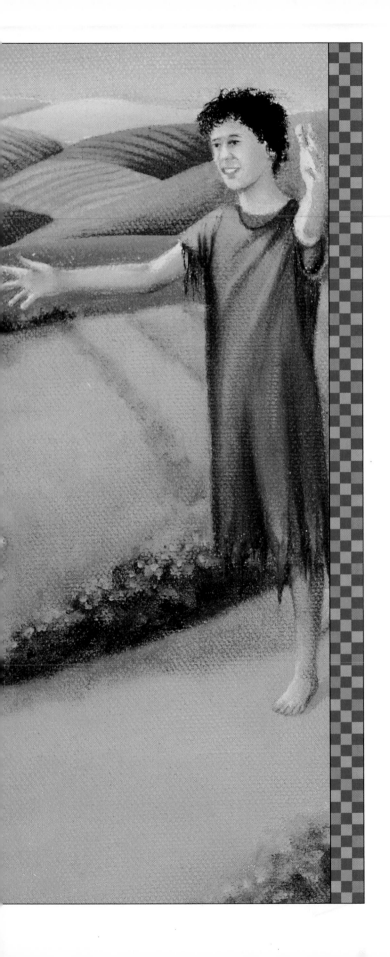

He began the long trip home. It took days and days, but finally he could see his father's house in the distance.

Ever since his younger son left, the father had watched for him, hoping he would come home. When he saw his son walking down the road toward him, he could hardly believe his eyes! He ran to greet him and to welcome him home.

"Father," said the son, "I'm sorry. I know I've been foolish. I know I made you sad. I don't deserve to be your son anymore, but please let me be a servant here."

To show that he forgave his son, the father called his servants and said, "Quickly, bring out a robe—the best one—and put it on him. Put a ring on his finger and sandals on his feet."

Then the father ordered that a great feast be prepared to celebrate his younger son's return.

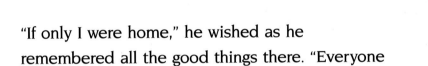

"If only I were home," he wished as he remembered all the good things there. "Everyone eats well. Even the servants have plenty to eat."

He missed his father and brother very much. But he was afraid to go home. What if his father didn't love him anymore?

Finally he decided, "I will return home and tell my father that I know I was wrong and I'm very sorry. If he'll forgive me, maybe he will at least let me be a servant in his house."

When the older son came home from the fields that night,
he heard the music and asked what the celebration was for.
A servant said, "Your brother has returned home and your

father is thrilled. He is having a party."

The older brother was so angry he would not go into the house.

The father came out to see what was wrong.

"How could you have a party for the son who left you and spent all the money you gave him?" the older brother asked. "All these years I have worked for you, and yet you never had a party for me."

Understanding his older son's feelings, the father gently explained, "Son, you are always with me and everything I have is yours. Your brother made a mistake, but he is sorry and has come home. We thought he was dead, but he is alive and has come back to us. How can we not celebrate and be happy?"

The younger son came out from the house and joined his family. He was thankful to be back home with his father and brother.

"I am a happy man," said the father. "Both of the sons I love very much are with me. Now my family is together once again."

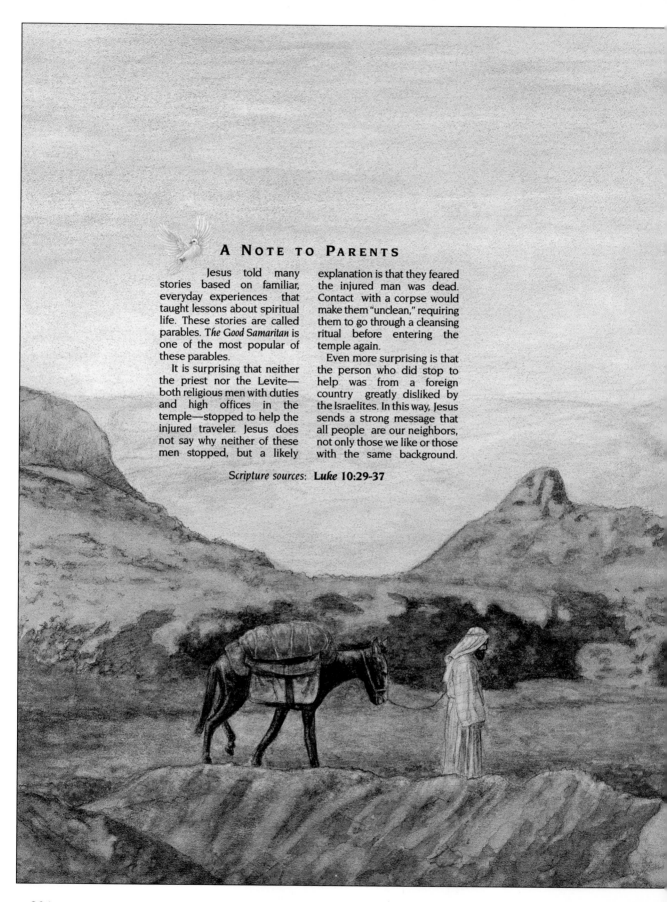

A NOTE TO PARENTS

Jesus told many stories based on familiar, everyday experiences that taught lessons about spiritual life. These stories are called parables. *The Good Samaritan* is one of the most popular of these parables.

It is surprising that neither the priest nor the Levite—both religious men with duties and high offices in the temple—stopped to help the injured traveler. Jesus does not say why neither of these men stopped, but a likely explanation is that they feared the injured man was dead. Contact with a corpse would make them "unclean," requiring them to go through a cleansing ritual before entering the temple again.

Even more surprising is that the person who did stop to help was from a foreign country greatly disliked by the Israelites. In this way, Jesus sends a strong message that all people are our neighbors, not only those we like or those with the same background.

Scripture sources: **Luke 10:29-37**

THE GOOD SAMARITAN

Retold by Jane Q. Saxton

Illustrated by Robert Casilla

Jesus often traveled with his disciples and talked about God. He told stories about love and forgiveness.

One day a lawyer asked Jesus, "Teacher, how should I live my life?"

"What are God's rules?" asked Jesus.

"You must love God and love your neighbor," said the lawyer.

"Yes," said Jesus.

"But teacher," the lawyer asked, "who is my neighbor?"

Jesus told him the story that follows.

One day a man was walking alone along a dusty, narrow road that led away from Jerusalem.

Suddenly, robbers jumped out at the man. They beat him up
and stole his money and clothes. Then the robbers ran away.

They left the man lying in the road. He was so badly hurt that
he could not even move.

Soon a priest, who was also
traveling from Jerusalem,
came down the road. He saw
the hurt man lying there.

But the priest did not stop to help the hurt man. He thought the
man was probably dead.

The priest did not want to touch him. He hurried past the hurt
man and went on his way.

Later a Levite came along on the same road. He, too, saw the hurt man lying there.

But the Levite did not stop to help either. He was much too busy. He hurried past the hurt man and went on his way.

Then a man traveling from the country of Samaria came down the road. He saw the hurt man lying there.

Would the Samaritan feel sorry for the hurt man?

Would the Samaritan stop and help him?

Yes, the Samaritan did stop. He gave the hurt man a drink.

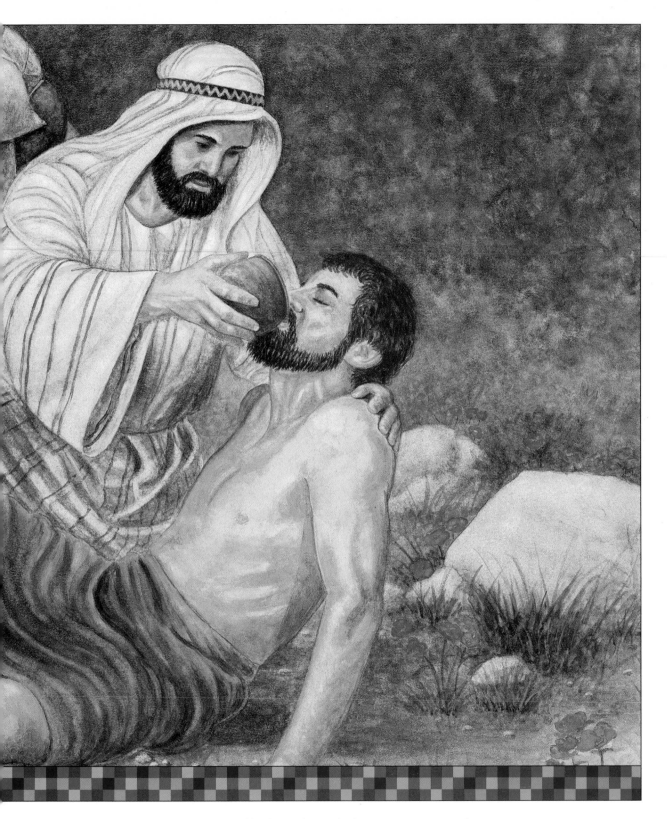

Then he carefully bandaged the man's wounds.

The Samaritan gently lifted the man onto his donkey and took him to an inn.

"Please take good care of this man. He has been badly injured," said the Samaritan to the innkeeper. He gave money to the innkeeper to pay for his help. "I will visit him again. And I will give you more money when I return."

When Jesus finished he said, "Three people in this story saw the man who had been hurt by robbers."

Then Jesus asked, "Who was loving and helpful? Who was a neighbor to the hurt man?"

"The Samaritan," the lawyer answered.

"Yes," said Jesus.

Then Jesus raised his hands to the crowd and
said, "All people are your neighbors. Be kind
to everyone. Be loving and helpful in big and
in small ways. Be like the good Samaritan."

A NOTE TO PARENTS

The story of Easter is at the heart of the Christian faith. For children, though, Jesus' resurrection may not seem like a miracle since children often have trouble comprehending the finality of death. To help them relate to the Easter story, share experiences with new or renewed life: plant a bulb and watch it grow; search for a new sprout or bud from a dormant plant; marvel over baby animals. Very young children may not understand the symbolism, but they can enjoy the experiences and later relate them to the resurrection.

We chose not to include the crucifixion with the Easter story. You can explain to young children that some of Jesus' enemies killed him, but God did not let Jesus stay dead. We call the day that he died "Good Friday" because we know of the joy to come on Easter Sunday.

Scripture sources: **Matthew 28:1-10 and 16-20; Luke 24:50-53**

THE MIRACLE OF EASTER

Retold by Terrell D. Smith

Illustrated by Arvis Stewart

Early one Sunday morning a long time ago,
the sun was just beginning to peek over the
horizon. It was the dawn of a very happy day.
It was the very first Easter morning.

Just outside the city of Jerusalem was the place where Jesus had died and been buried. Weary soldiers guarded his tomb.

On this first Easter morning, God sent an angel to bring happy news to Jesus' friends. Jesus was no longer dead! He had been brought back to life.

The soldiers standing guard outside the tomb where Jesus was
buried were startled to feel the earth shake beneath their feet.

They turned to see the angel easily rolling the huge stone away from the entrance to the tomb.

The soldiers were scared when they saw the angel. Some fell down, and some turned and ran away.

Jesus' friends Mary
Magdalene and another
woman named Mary were on
their way to Jesus' tomb
when they felt the ground
trembling as if there were an
earthquake. What could it
be? They were scared and
ran to the tomb.

When the two frightened women reached the tomb, they saw that
the big stone had been rolled away. To their amazement, on top of

the stone sat an angel. He was as bright as lightning and his clothes
were as white as snow.

The angel said to them, "Do not be afraid. Jesus is not here. He has risen from the dead as he promised he would. You will see him again soon."

The women looked into the tomb and saw that the angel was right. Jesus' body was gone! All that was left was the white cloth that had been wrapped around his body.

Then the angel said, "Go quickly and tell the disciples that the tomb is empty. Jesus has risen. He is alive. You will see him again."

What a wonderful day! Jesus was not dead!

The women ran from the tomb to find the disciples. Along the way, they saw a familiar-looking figure ahead of them. When they got closer, they realized who it was. It was their friend and teacher, Jesus!

"Peace be with you," Jesus said warmly.

The women kneeled down at Jesus' feet and worshiped him.

"Go and tell my disciples they will see me soon," he told them.

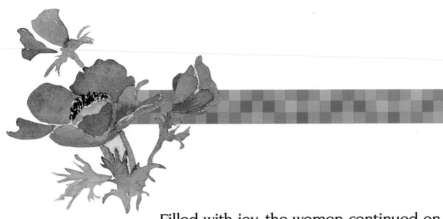

Filled with joy, the women continued on to
find the disciples and tell them they had seen Jesus.
"He is risen! He is risen!" they shouted happily.

Later Jesus appeared to the disciples.

He told them, "Go to all the people everywhere and teach them what I have taught you about love and forgiveness. And remember, I will always be with you."

Jesus raised his hands and blessed the disciples, then rose to heaven.

Time-Life Books is a division of Time Life, Inc.

TIME-LIFE CUSTOM PUBLISHING

VICE PRESIDENT *and* PUBLISHER: Terry Newell
Associate Publisher: Teresa Hartnett
Vice President of Sales and Marketing: Neil Levin
Project Manager: Jennifer M. Lee
Director of Special Sales: Liz Ziehl
Managing Editor: Donia Steele
Production Manager: Carolyn Clark
Quality Assurance Manager: Miriam P. Newton

"A Note to Parents" written for each story by Delia Halverson, consultant for
Family Time Bible Stories. An interdenominational lecturer on religious
education, she has written nine books, including *How Do Our Children Grow?*

Stories in this book previously published in the series *Family Time Bible Stories*.

Deputy Editors:	Patricia Daniels	*Produced by*:	Kirchoff/Wohlberg, Inc.
	Terrell D. Smith		866 United Nations Plaza
			New York, NY 10017

First printing. Printed in U.S.A.
TIME-LIFE is a trademark of Time Warner Inc. U.S.A.

School and library distribution by Time-Life Education, P.O. Box 85026, Richmond, VA 23285-5026.
For subscription information, call 1-800-621-7026.

Library of Congress Cataloging-in-Publication Data

Children's Favorite Bible Stories / by the Editors of Time-Life Books.
p. cm.
Contents: In the Beginning /retold by Mary Quattlebaum — Adam and Eve/retold by Mary Martin — Noah's Ark/retold by Patrica Daniels — Joseph and the Coat of Many Colors/retold by Andrew Gutelle — David and Goliath/retold by Andrew Gutelle — Jonah and the Whale/retold by Melissa Nichols — The Story of Baby Jesus/retold by Patricia Daniels — The Prodigal Son/retold by David Michaels — The Good Samaritan/retold by Jane Q. Saxton — The Miracle of Easter/retold by Terrell D. Smith.
ISBN: 0-7835-4925-3
1. Bible Stories, English.   [1. Bible stories.]   I. Time-Life Books.
BS551.2.C48 1997   96-54249
220.9'505—dc21   CIP
                                                            AC